TEENAGERS ARE AWESOME

You Just Have to Get to Know Them

Ali Baksh

Teenagers Are Awesome, You Just Have to Get to Know Them
www.myworldisbetter.com

Copyright © 2018 Ali Baksh

ISBN: 978-1-77277-227-2

All rights reserved. No portion of this book may be reproduced mechanically, electronically, or by any other means, including photocopying, without permission of the publisher or author except in the case of brief quotations embodied in critical articles and reviews. It is illegal to copy this book, post it to a website, or distribute it by any other means without permission from the publisher or author.

Limits of Liability and Disclaimer of Warranty
The author and publisher shall not be liable for your misuse of the enclosed material. This book is strictly for informational and educational purposes only.

Warning – Disclaimer
The purpose of this book is to educate and entertain. The author and/or publisher do not guarantee that anyone following these techniques, suggestions, tips, ideas, or strategies will become successful. The author and/or publisher shall have neither liability nor responsibility to anyone with respect to any loss or damage caused, or alleged to be caused, directly or indirectly by the information contained in this book.

Medical Disclaimer
The medical or health information in this book is provided as an information resource only, and is not to be used or relied on for any diagnostic or treatment purposes. This information is not intended to be patient education, does not create any patient-physician relationship, and should not be used as a substitute for professional diagnosis and treatment.

Published by the 10-10-10 program
First Edition 2018

Printed in Canada and the United States of America

Table of Contents

Dedication	v
Foreword	vii
Acknowledgements	ix

Chapter 1
What Teens Want vs What Teens Need   1

Chapter 2
How to Understand a Teenager   17

Chapter 3
Things You Should Teach Your Teen   31

Chapter 4
How Teens Thrive in Their Everyday Life   55

Chapter 5
Why Teens Are So Awesome   67

Chapter 6
How Teens Will Change the World   79

Bonus Chapter
What Do You Want To Be?   89

About the Book   99
About the Author   101

Dedication

I would like to dedicate this book to my family, and the people who helped me create this book.

Foreword

Ali Baksh is an amazing young man. At only 12 years of age, he has written his first book, *Teenagers Are Awesome*, just for you!

Today, you and I live in an era, where opportunities are rare, suicide is far too prevalent, and where you as a teenager may not get along with your parents. *Teenagers Are Awesome*, by Ali Baksh, can help you through these struggles in life, and help you realize that anything is possible, even in dark times. Ali talks about how to deal with situations in the best possible way, so that your parents can build a bond with you, and he gives some practical advice about how to get a job.

Sadly, every 100 minutes a teen commits suicide because of depression. Many teens around the world are unemployed until they are in their mid-twenties, and every day parents regret not paying enough attention to their teens, and not building a strong enough bond with them.

Ali has written this book for you, so that you can enjoy your life as a teen, help your parents get to know you better, and live an awesome life!

Raymond Aaron
New York Times Bestselling Author

Acknowledgements

I want to thank my mom, dad, grandma, grandpa, aunts, uncles, cousins, my sister, and my friend, Chinmai Swamy, and Raymond Aaron. I want to thank my mom for being an amazing person who has helped me throughout my life, and who always said that I would be successful. My dad, thank you for being a great father and for teaching me how to be tough in times of hardship. My grandma, thank you for being a great person who always makes me laugh, and who never gave up on me. My grandpa, thank you for always teaching a new lesson, each day of my life, even if you don't realize that you are teaching me, you do so without even knowing. My aunt and uncle, thank you for always giving me snacks and food when I came over on my bike rides, because those snacks gave me extra power so I could finish this book. My cousins, Ajay R. and Lana C.: To Ajay, thank you for being a great cousin. I look up to you because of your style and your academic success. To Lana, thank you for always bringing out the happiness in me, and even if you don't understand what I'm saying right now, I know that you understand that I love you. To my sister, thank you for helping throughout my life, even when I annoy you every day, 24/7. You always have the kindness in your heart to let me do that. Thank you for helping me with this book, and for always having my back when I need it most. To my friend, Angie, I thank you for being a great friend to me when I need it the most. Thank you also for telling me that I would finish this book. To Chinmai Swamy, thank you for being a great mentor who is always happy, and for never giving up on me. To Raymond Aaron, where do I start? Thank you for being a role model for me, and for helping me sign up for this program that you created. Thank you for inviting me as a guest to come to your speaker master class, because I learned a lot there. Thank you for seeing the potential that I had, and for always giving me a smile when I was down. One last thing I forgot to say is, thank you to my

Acknowledgements

parents for investing so much money in my life, so that I can become a success. Don't worry; I will pay all the money back.

Chapter 1

What Teens Want vs What Teens Need

As a teen, I like many things. I have friends who are teenagers, and my sister is a teenager. What do teens like? I can't speak for everyone, but these are the things teens like, from my experience. Number one is sports; sports are something that most teens love. Personally, I love sports. Whenever I play sports, I block out everything around me and solely focus on the game. That is one reason I'm so competitive when it comes to sports.

Number two is music. Music is something that most teens love. The most popular genre of music, in my opinion, is hip-hop. When my friends and I hang out, we always listen to hip-hop. Music greatly influences teenagers. Some songs make me feel happy, and some make me feel sad, but most of the time, the music makes me really happy; I start dancing to it, and then my sister comes, and we have a great time.

Number 3 is shopping. Shopping is something that I know the majority of teens like. Most of the clothing stores get most of their income from teenagers and young adults. When teens go shopping, they plan on buying one thing, but they end up coming out with 5 bags. One of my friends went to LA and spent $25,000 in one day. When I see something I want, I buy it with my own money. Whenever I go shopping, I look for things that are trending, but when it comes to shoes, I buy what I want to buy, and I don't listen to what other people think.

Number four is concerts. I know as a teen, I love music, and when I see that one of my favorite artists is coming to Toronto, I want to go and see their concert right away. I never get to because I am too young. Many teens spend lots of money on concerts, just so they can see their favorite artists; that's how much they love music.

Number 5 is phones and apps. I love my phone, and so do millions of other teens. When I get my phone taken away, I get mad; but then I realize I actually do not need it at all. Too many teens around the world are addicted to their phones, and it is not healthy for them. Some apps that teenagers are addicted to are Snapchat, Instagram, and any other social media app. Some teenagers will constantly check their phone, just to see if they have lost a follower on Instagram. Social media apps have literally been taking over teenagers' lives, even though social media sometimes can be a gateway for freedom.

Freedom is something that I want, because I want to be able to explore the world. I know that my parents are very protective of my sister and I and that they don't want us to get hurt in any way. When I was younger, I wasn't allowed to go outside alone because my parents didn't want anything to happen to me. This year, my parents have finally given me some freedom, so I can go and do some stuff that I want. Of course, there are some rules, though; one of them being that I have to be home before 9 p.m. I can't go too far without my sister, and I must take water with me so I don't dehydrate.

I love my parents so much, and that's why I understand when they don't let me go out and do stuff without my sister; they're just trying to protect me. If your parents are like this, try to understand where they're coming from. If you live in a neighborhood where there's a lot of danger and crime, and things like that, and your parents won't let you go out, try to understand that you don't live in an extremely safe place. If you lived in a nice neighborhood, and it was really safe, but your parents still wouldn't let you have much freedom...well, maybe they're just extremely protective of you.

What Teens Want vs What Teens Need

If you are a parent, and you are reading this: if teenagers have too much freedom, then you have a problem on your hands. Over the years of my life, I have known some people that have had a lot of freedom, and they ended up getting into a lot of trouble. So, if you are going to let your teen have some freedom—to go out to the mall with their friends, or go to movies, or things like that—remember to set rules so they don't go off and do crazy things, and then get in trouble. This might seem like a rant to you, but I'm telling you these things because I don't want you to get in trouble doing dumb things that you know you weren't supposed to be doing.

Allowing a teenager some freedom is something they need in order for them to grow in a very healthy way. If you keep your teen locked up in the house how is your teen supposed to explore the world ? That's why I'm writing about freedom; because that is something I want, so that I can explore the world in my own way, and experience different things. Some of my friends' parents give their children lots and lots of freedom because they trust them. My parents trust my sister and me because we have built that trust up.

Freedom is something that every single person on Earth deserves. Many people do not get freedom, because the people protecting them are afraid that they're going to get involved in bad things. I knew somebody who had lots of freedom, and they ended up getting involved with drugs and a whole bunch of other things like that; and to this point, I don't know how they're doing. I'm telling you these stories because, if you're reading my book, I don't want you to get involved in problems that you can't get out of. I want you to live a good life, while having freedom, but if you don't use that freedom wisely, you could get your freedom taken away in a split second. For example, people in jail did something stupid. Now they are confined to a small space, and their freedom has been taken away. Sometimes you may make mistakes in life; but don't worry, I know that you can fix it.

Being a teenager, I know I make mistakes a lot. I make mistakes over and over again, and I still don't learn from them. I have been in trouble many times and, in some cases, I only get one chance. When I was in grade 3, 4, or maybe 5, my teachers would say, "Okay, this is your first warning." Well, in the real world, you only get one chance, and if you have already messed up that chance, I'm going to tell you how to get a second chance— make sure you use this second chance wisely.

If you are applying for a job, and you get a job interview, but you blow it, don't spend too much time thinking about it and getting frustrated. The first thing you should do is write an email and send it to the employer and tell them why you messed up. They might give you a second chance, because they are human. If you blew it with your parents because you got into a big fight or argument, or something like that, and you messed up big-time, I can't really help you on that. I don't know your parents and how they react to certain things, but from my experience, how I get second chances is to work for it by doing things for them, and to I say I'm sorry, and explain why I did what I did. I usually tell them I love them, and then everything is okay for me, but I don't know how it goes for you with your parents.

So, I told you how to get a second chance for a job, and with your parents, but now I'm going to tell you how to get opportunities in the world. I can't physically get you opportunities, but I can give you tips, though, to help you get opportunities. My experience, at the age of 13, is that I can't get many opportunities; but from my experiences, I have seen other people get good opportunities because of certain tips that I'm about to tell you.

The first tip I'm going to give you is, when you see an opening for a job, maybe from an ad or a hiring sign, and if it's something that you're interested in, take it right away. A wise person once told me that opportunities don't come to you—you have to chase opportunities if you want them. The second tip I have for you is, when you get your opportunity, you have to make a decision right away. You either take it or you leave it. If it's something that you love a lot, but it doesn't pay enough, then think really hard for a second. What is better? Something that you enjoy but with little pay, or something that you hate but with big pay? A way to find opportunities for a job, or for volunteering in something that you love, is to look it up on Google. Yes, this is a very simple thing, and you probably tried, but try again—do it over and over again. Don't give up until you really feel that you can't do it anymore; and if you feel like that, then say no, but continue to do it over and over.

As a teenager, I want *trust*. Whether the trust is with my parents, or with my friends, I want trust. The trust that I want the most is with my parents. I want to be able to trust my parents that they won't go snooping around in my stuff, and that they can trust me to go out by myself and explore the world. I want them to be able to trust me with money. As a teenager, I can't just get things that I want; I have to work for it, but that's okay. I know that I have to build up that trust with them before they can trust me. I might build up their trust by doing things around the house, helping my parents with things they need. I would do anything to build up trust with my parents.

Throughout our entire childhood, my sister and I were never allowed to go outside, or to places, without an adult. My parents didn't trust the people outside. So, for the first time, my sister and I are finally allowed to go places without them. We have built trust with our parents so that they can trust us to go places and come back home safe, with no problems. Another type of trust I build with my parents is when they give us money to do go things, they can trust us to give them back their change. So my sister and I do this, and that is how we build trust with them. You may want to know how I get money. Well, like I said before, I do stuff around the house. I help them clean, and do all sorts of things. When you build trust with your parents, they will start to let you do things that you weren't allowed do before.

When I make new friends, from the first moment on, I make a bond with my friend; and that's how I know I can trust them. I have to be very careful with the people I talk to because I don't trust some of them, and that's why I don't tell them stuff. They might complain and whine about why I don't tell them anything—and then I say, "Well, you're a snitch." If you are in a relationship, then trust is one of the most important things. When you trust somebody, you're telling them that you think they are a reliable person, that you have confidence in them, and that you feel comfortable, both physically and emotionally, around that person. In my own opinion, I believe that without trust, nobody can get anywhere in this world today. If you are in a job, and you get something assigned to you, your boss is trusting you with that assignment. He/she has faith that you will get it done.

The last thing I want to say is that when someone trusts you, you better keep that trust because, if not, then you could lose your job, relationship, or friendship with someone you really care about, just because you broke their trust. I know, because I have lost someone's trust by accident before, and it took me many months for them to trust me again. Trust is the thing that I believe is keeping this world together. Without trust, our world would fall apart. Some examples would be, if the government didn't trust each other, our world would be back to the Stone Age. If countries couldn't trust one another, then we would be at war. Trust is the most important thing, for all of us to live a happy life.

What Teens Want vs What Teens Need

Notes

Notes

What Teens Want vs What Teens Need

Notes

Teenagers are Awesome

Notes

Chapter 2

How to Understand a Teenager

There are many ways to communicate with a teen. When you communicate with a teen, you have to act calm and just act normal. One thing that I hate the most is when my parents try to act cool and start saying *dude*, *bro*, or things like that, or if they use emojis. I hate when they do this because it's not like them. I know, nowadays, parents are trying to feel young again by using emojis and things like that, but I have one tip for you: stick to your jobs please. *I'm just joking.* If you are a parent, do anything you want to do.

Getting back to the topic, how to communicate with teens, you should listen before you jump in and start yelling and screaming. Yes, I'm still talking about parents. If you are a parent, and you are trying to get your teen to open up to you, some ways to get this to happen are to listen to what they have to say, do not interrupt them while they are talking to you, do not judge them, do not give them a lecture (until they are finished talking to you, but try not to give lectures at all, whether they are talking to you or not), and most important, if they are talking to you, do not interrupt. These are just some of the tips that I think will help you to get your teen to open up.

As a teenager, I know that you are under a lot of pressure: from school, trying to fit in, or from pretty much anything you do. Now, if you are a parent, I know that you probably want to help your teen under this pressure. It has been shown that when you leave a teenager under pressure, it's actually good for them. This might sound a little weird, so let me explain it better. When a teenager is under pressure, it helps them to become stronger and more independent; it teaches them how to become more organized, and teaches them how to follow a schedule, and many other things.

If you are a parent, this might be really hard, but do not try to help your teen; just acknowledge that they are going through pain so that when they are in their mid-twenties, and this comes back on them in university, or at a job, they will know how to survive under pressure. A fun fact about this is when teenagers are under stress and are going through pain, it helps to develop their prefrontal cortex.

During the school year, or in the summer, I'm always on my phone or on my computer; and most of the time, I'm not even doing anything. I'm just watching videos or talking to friends, and doing a whole bunch of other things I don't really need to be doing. So, what do you think my parents do? My parents take my phone away, or they tell me to get off of it, and they yell at me to do my homework. They tell me to stay on top of my stuff—and you know what? I think it helps me, because I start to focus more on whatever I'm doing.

Apparently, nowadays, parents should not take their teens' phones away, but this surprised me when I heard it. They should just teach their teens how to limit their selves with their phones and computers games, as well as with all sorts of other things, so that they don't need to actually take the phones away. See, I understand that now; but I'm not about to tell my parents, because they would think that's a silly idea. Another reason my parents would take my phone and computer away would be because I'm on it way too long, and *it's damaging my eyes*, and *that's why I have to wear glasses*. I'm not going to tell you why I have glasses, but the truth is, it's not because of my games.

Getting back to earlier, when I said you shouldn't intervene when your teen is going through a whole bunch of problems, and pain, and things like that—if you have already intervened, and you yelled at them, or you didn't listen to them, and you just kept lecturing them over and over again—then next time, if you do that, you should just put yourself in their shoes. What I mean by that is, if you were a teenager, and you were going through what they are going through, how would you feel if your parent was yelling at you, and you just got a lecture, over and over again? How would you feel if you were the teenager?

You would probably feel like your parents don't understand you. I have actually witnessed this a lot of times, where a parent would just yell at their child, and say, "Why aren't you doing good in school? Why aren't you doing this, and why aren't you doing that?" I would see the teenager just standing there, silent, not doing anything. And the parents wonder why the teen is still not doing well. *Maybe it's because you just yelled at them, lectured them, and put them down. Maybe it's because you made them feel like you don't like them.*

So, the next time, before you start yelling at your teenager over and over again, make sure you put yourself in their shoes, and listen to what they have to say. Say something afterwards, but make sure you do not start ranting and lecturing them after you have listened, because then it just diminishes the point of listening to them. If you are parents, and you feel like your teen doesn't spend enough time with the family, you should take action and ask them what they want to do. If they say they want to go back on their phone and play games and stuff, you just need to say, "No, come on, let's do something that you like." If they like shopping, you could say, "Okay, let's go shopping," or, if they like playing basketball, you could say, "Let's go play a game of basketball." Doing things like this will help create a stronger bond between you and your teenager.

You might say, "Oh yeah, that's simple enough." But actually, many parents, all over the world, do not connect enough with their teens; and when the teens go off on their own, they don't have a strong bond with their parents. They didn't have a chance to get to know each other. And if something were to happen to the parents, or to the teenager, they would regret not spending time with each other. So, that's why I'm telling you that you need to create a bond with your teen—as soon as you can.

If you reached this point, you will see that I have taught you how to communicate with your teen properly, and how intervening a teen's problem can impact them. Now I'm going to teach you how to deal with problems in the right way. When my parents and I get into arguments, it usually ends up with me getting sent to my room and getting my phone taken away. What is it that I get in trouble for? I usually get in trouble because I either did bad on a spelling test, I did bad in school, I got into a fight, or I got into a big argument with one of my family members, or pretty much whenever I talk back to any one of my parents or grandparents, or my sister.

The next question I have to answer is how my parents deal with the problems. Depending on how big it is, ranging from me talking back, to me swearing, it can get pretty serious. If I talk back, I usually just get yelled at and get told to go to my room, or something like that. Even though I'm a teenager, I still get sent to my room. If I swear, it can get pretty serious. My parents get really mad, because they're from a country where that is really normal. My parents listen to what I say, and understand sometimes. My mom listens to me more than my dad, because my dad is a little stubborn. Don't get me wrong; my dad and I have a very strong bond. We do lots of things together, like playing sports, watching movies, and watching TV shows, and we even go golfing sometimes, and that's really fun too.

If your teen is getting really depressed, and you end up intervening, and yelling and screaming and cursing at them, you put their self-esteem down to pretty much nothing. So, what do you do after you have yelled at them and put their self-esteem down? Do you feel terrible and try to fix your mistake? How do you do that? You can say that you are sorry. If your teen is depressed, or they're having problems, but you're not sure how they feel, then ask them how they feel. I know I'm repeating myself over and over again, but this is crucial. If you don't ask your teen how they feel, they'll never open up to you. Remember, you have to listen—don't go off on a rant, giving them a lecture—just listen to what they have to say. Ask them how they feel, and once they are done, then you can respond to what they have said. You can also explain yourself to them, about why you got mad. If they talk back to you, you still have to listen to what they're saying, for them to feel like you actually care.

Try to comfort your teen when they need it most. As a parent, you might not see right away when your teen is in trouble or when something has happened. They won't tell you right away because they're afraid of the consequences that will come after they tell you. So, when you sit down and talk to them, and you listen to what they have to say, if they start crying or tell you something really deep, start to comfort them by hugging them and telling them that you love them. Let them know that everything is going to be okay, and see what happens next. When my parents and I get into a fight, they do a pretty good job of comforting me afterwards. They explain why they said what they said, and why they yelled at me. Then, I explain everything to them in a way that they will understand.

How to Understand a Teenager

Notes

Teenagers are Awesome

Notes

Notes

Notes

Chapter 3

Things You Should Teach Your Teen

This is my favourite topic. Today, I'm going to teach you the tricks of the trade. When I don't want to do something, I either trick someone else into doing it or I find a short cut in doing that thing. An example is, when I don't want to do my chores, I will pay my sister do it, and I only pay her $2, but she does it. Another example is, if someone owes me money, and I have to get something done, I will offer to pay them the amount of money they owe me; and then, when they are finished, I will tell them that I don't pay them because they owed me. When I'm reading a novel for school, and I am asked to answer questions, I don't actually read the book. I scan the book to look for the answers.

I know that when I grow up, I want to work hard and smart at the same time. You might not understand, so let me break it down. When I get employed, I'm going to work hard, but I'm going to work in a smart way, so that I don't have to be stressed out. I want to be successful, so I'm going to work hard in the short term, and work smart in the long term. Here are some ways to become more productive: take more breaks so your brain can relax, because you work long hours at school; follow the 80/20 rule; focus on yourself in the morning; do the hard tasks before lunch; and create a system.

The first thing you may be wondering is, what is the 80/20 rule? The 80/20 rule is also called the *Pareto Principle*. It was named after its founder, Vilfredo Pareto, back in 1895. The 80/20 rule suggests that 20% of your activities will account for 80% of your results. Secondly, you may be wondering what I mean by focusing on yourself in the morning. I'm saying that instead of getting up and looking at your phone, checking Instagram and snapchat, just forget about those things—work out, sleep in, read a book, and make sure you have a healthy breakfast, so you can start your day off in the right way.

Creating a system may be hard, but I know that you can do it. Here is a simple way that you can create a system that can help you. The first thing is to write down what you have to do today, from first thing in the morning to the afternoon. And remember to put breaks in there so your brain has time to relax. Also, if you have something to do in the morning, around 8:15 and on, wake up a little bit earlier so you can work out, and have a great breakfast. When you start doing all of these things, you will realize that you are getting better grades in school, and if you are working, then maybe you will start seeing more money come in, with less stress. The last thing I want to say is, when you are in school, I'm not saying you should not work hard. You need to work hard, and smart. An example is, when exams come around, and you get your exam review sheet, study each page. Each day, study a different page, and then go over them, over and over, till exams come around. With each day you study, you will pick up some hardworking traits, one of which can be determination.

Determination is what drives me to do my best. It forces me to do better than the rest, and it pushes me to keep going when I want to give up. Determination works best.

Being a teenager, I know that when I want to get something done, determination drives me to finish what I am doing. When I do track and field, determination forces me to do better than the rest, because I know that I don't want to be last. I follow one rule: **MTO**.

What does **MTO** stand for? **M** stands for minimum; **T** stands for Target; and **O** stands for outrageous. I was told about this rule by one of the most famous speakers in the world—Raymond Aaron. Raymond Aaron told me this because I had a goal that I wasn't sure if I could meet. He told me this, and then determination kicked in, and that is how I met my goal.

I have a story that I'm going to tell you. It was the year 2016, sometime in June. My school and I we're at Varsity Stadium in Toronto. It was the last race of the day, and I was the only one in my class doing it: the 200-meter race. I had been running all day, doing all sorts of other track and field events, and this was the last one of the day—I was so tired. It was my turn, and I was getting ready to run the 200m race, with no energy left inside of me. The buzzer went off, and I started running as fast as I could. I was getting so tired, so I started dropping back. Then I heard everybody chanting: "Come on, you can do it! You can do it!" And then I started running as fast as I could again. I ran so fast, because of determination. I was determined to finish in the top three spots, and you know what? I placed second in that race. I went from being last place, all the way to finishing second place, and I was just so happy—all because of something called *determination*.

You may be wondering why I told you that story. I told you that story because, from my experience, many people do not believe in determination. I told you that story for you to see that determination is a real thing, and if you put your mind to it, determination will take over, and you will accomplish whatever you want to do. Another example of determination is my sister. You have heard this story already, but I'm going to tell you one more time so you can see how determined she was to accomplish her goal. In both grades 9 and 10, my sister was so determined to pass math that she went from 38% to 82%. You might be wondering how she did that, and I'm going to tell you. My sister was so determined to pass math that she worked her butt off the entire summer. No matter what got in her way, she just kept pushing through it, because something inside of her—something called determination—popped out and said, "You are passing math," and you know what? That's how she passed the math class—all because of determination.

Now you have read about two examples of determination that I have experienced in my life: the first one being my track and field race, and the second one being my sister struggling in math, and then passing. If you are reading this, then the next time you think you cannot do something, remember what you are going to get out of it when you accomplish your goal. If you play sports, what do you think drives you to do your best? Determination. If you're studying for exams, and you know that you're going to fail, what pushes you to continue studying? Determination. If you are practicing for what is going to be a big day for you, and you are feeling really nervous that you won't be able to do it, what do you think pushes you to go up and do it? Determination. When you are determined to do something, everything will become much easier for you. That is why I want you to be determined to complete your goal—no matter what.

I am a teen, and I think I know everything, but that's not the case. I actually do not know as much as I think I know. Something that I actually would love to learn, which school doesn't teach, is how to budget money, how to spend money, and just money skills in general. The school system teaches you how to become an employee, but it does not teach you how to save your money, or how to use your money wisely, and it does not teach you how to invest your money. In other words, school does not teach you anything about budgeting or money skills, so that's why it's up to the parents to teach their teens these skills. Without these money skills, I know I'm not going to have a comfortable life. I won't know how to save money, and I won't know how to invest it or to make more money outside of being employed.

Another thing I would love to learn is how to cook. Learning how to cook is an essential thing for a healthy life. If you do not know how to cook, then you're mostly going to be eating instant food, or you are going to go out and buy lots of food that is not healthy for you. You may become overweight, and get a whole bunch of health problems, but if you learn how to cook, then you can live a healthy life. You'll make healthier choices and lead a healthier life.

Another thing that I have witnessed over the years is cleanliness and hygiene. If you are a parent, and you are reading this book, teach your teenager how to vacuum. Teach them to mop floors, keep the bathroom clean, clean the kitchen, take out garbage regularly, and eliminate clutter from their desk and their room. All those things teach them how to become more organized and clean. You also need to teach them about their hygiene. If you do not teach them these things, then they're going to be living in a dump for the rest of their life, and they're going to have to learn the hard way.

Another essential thing that you should know as a teen is basic first aid knowledge. Knowing this could possibly save your life or somebody else's life. Just knowing how to call 911, and how to stay calm in certain situations, could save your life or someone else's.

I know for a fact that I do not have proper organization skills. I tend to lose things, and then I get in trouble for losing these things. If you are a parent, teach your kids how to organize properly. Teach them how to eliminate clutter in the room so that it makes it easier for them to find their things, and so that it doesn't take up as much of their time. Explain to them how to organize their desk in a certain way, or their room, so that they can find things easier and faster. They won't be wasting time trying to find something that is right in front of their face.

When I get my driver's license, I want to be able to go all over the place, but I can't do that if I don't have any navigation skills. Sure, there might be a GPS built into the car, but what if that does not work? I have to use maps. I know how to read maps, and get from point A to point B, but many teens do not actually know. One of my friends, for example, didn't know how to get from my house to the grocery store, without getting lost or using their phone to help them get there. If you're getting your driver's license, you need to know these basic things: right, left, north, south, east, and west. If you want to get around, you have to know this. It can save you time, and from getting stuck in traffic. If you're getting your driver's license, one of the most basic navigation skills you will need, if you're going to go on long trips, is how to read signs. Having a knowledge of traffic and road terms will help you a lot when you are driving.

Last but not least, I want to know about problem-solving. Yes, I know that school teachers know how to problem-solve, but in my experience, when I come across something that I actually have to use my brain for, I don't know how to do it. This is why I want my parents to teach me how to face problems, and to take care of them quickly. I would like to just be able to use the knowledge that I have, so that I don't have to actually look it up. I want to be able to get problems over and done with, so I don't have to face it again.

Don't judge a book by its cover.

You may have heard of this saying before, but do you know what it means? The idiom is a metaphorical phrase that is saying that you should not prejudge something by its outer appearance. An example is, if you go to Chapters, and you see a book with a black cover and nothing else but a title, you will most likely not pick it up, because it is plain—but you might have just missed out on a lot of knowledge, because that book was all about how to become rich in a couple of days. See, now you have missed out on how to be rich. Every day, millions of people get judged because of their outer appearance. They don't get a chance to show who they really are, so they end up trying to change their outer appearance. In high school, this happens every day, because people quickly judge others. I was at a workshop once, and the speaker there asked, "When a girl arrives at a party, how long do you think it takes for the guys to judge her?" The answer: "Less than one second."

I'm not trying to be rude, but that is how quickly people judge one another. A couple of years ago, there was a trend, where teens were taking pictures with homeless people, and making fun of them. I felt so bad for those homeless people because those teens were making fun of them, and they didn't even know what that person had been through. I'm going to be honest; I judge people very quickly based on how they look/dress, how they act, and finally, how they act toward me. I know that I should not do this because I'm not really giving people a chance, but if you're going to dress in ripped clothes, have a messy hairstyle, and approach me, thinking I'm going to like you, you're wrong, because you have not given a good impression. That is why one of my number one rules is to always dress your best.

If you don't always dress your best, or try to look your best, even if you're just going out to the mall, to the movies, or to Walmart, or anything like that, you should try to look your best, because you don't know how people will judge you. If you always act your best, dress your best, and treat people in the best way possible, you will be judged in a very good way; but if you're going to dress like a crazy person, you are going to get judged in a very bad way, and no one will get to know you for who you really are. Now, today, I give people chances. If they dress in a way that I do not like, I will still give them a chance, because I know they have probably been rejected over and over again, and they probably don't get chances. That is why I'm trying to change from my old behaviors to new behaviors, and that is why I'm telling you, if you see someone who may be depressed or looking sad, you should not just go up and say crap to them. Then you are just putting them down, and you won't get to know someone who could be amazing, just because you got the wrong impression of them.

Today, in our world, everybody is trying to be someone that they are not. Many people try to change themselves so they can fit the needs of someone else. Today, many people around the world are trying to be normal. I have one question, though: what is normal; what does normal mean? From my observations, I have seen that being different is being normal, and being normal is being different. You might not understand what I'm saying, so let me break it down for you. I am saying that if you're trying to change yourself, don't—because you are perfect in your own way. If you are someone who is trying to fit in, and you are saying that you just want to *be*, then stop— don't say you want to be normal, because you already are.

Being different and unique are amazing things, and if everybody in the world were to be all the same, the world would have over 7 billion people who were all the same. Now, would you want that. So I have a question: what do you want, to be unique and amazing, or to live in a world where everybody is the same? I know that I would not want to live in a world where no one is different, and that is why I am telling you that being different is being normal. When you are different, you are unique, and you're telling everybody that you are not the same—you are special. This is a big problem today because nobody wants to be themselves; everyone just wants to be like someone else. They say, "Oh, I wish I was rich; oh, I wish I had that; oh, I wish I had this; I wish I lived in a mansion; I wish I had a rich car; I wish I had a pool; I wish I could go on vacation."

If you say all these types of things, you are missing out on what is in front of you. You don't realize that you are alive; you don't realize that some people around the world have problems that they have to deal with. You're complaining because you want to be like someone else, while you have an amazing life, and you just don't realize it. You have to stop trying to act like someone else, and start acting like yourself. If you like art or math, or you like reading books, then do that. Don't let anyone tell you that you can't do that. If someone says Pokémon sucks, that's okay; don't let that get to you. Just say okay, and go on. Just because they said that they don't like Pokémon doesn't mean you don't have to like Pokémon. Don't let what anybody else tells you define who you are.

I know, in my life, I have said things that I probably shouldn't have, and I may have said those things because I was angry at the time. Now, I look back, and I say, "Why did I do that?" I have learned from my mistakes, and that is why I'm telling you that you should not change who you are. I tried doing that, and you know what? Halfway through, I said, "I can't do this. I'm amazing, I'm special, and I'm unique." There's an amazing poem that I learned in school, called *I Am*. There are many different ways in which this poem is written, but the one that I learned in school was the best one yet. I don't remember how it goes, but I can for sure tell you that it is different from the ones that you will find on Google. You can create your own "I Am" poem—it's easy. You start at the top, and you say, *I am*. Then, maybe, *I am amazing; I am funny; I am smart; I am unique; I am different.* Those are 5 right there. Then you might say 4 nouns: *I am a chef; I am a doctor; I am a cousin to blank; I am a student.*

Right there, there's 4. Then you will say 3 words that describe you: *I am strong; I am amazing; I am the best.* Then, for the last line, you would say, *I Am Me.*

There are so many things in the world that you can do besides trying to change yourself for someone else. This might have been a little boring for you, but I want you to know that you should never change yourself for anyone. That is my only message. I don't want you to change yourself. I want you to stay the way that you are because you are the best version of yourself, and you don't have change anything about yourself to fit someone else's needs. Just stay yourself, and you will have a happy life. Don't let anybody push you around; don't let anything bother you—just live your life.

Living Life to the Fullest

This is something that I want to know as a teen, because I don't want to live my life sitting at a desk 24/7, helping other people, when I can't even help myself. I want to live a life where I can have freedom and do whatever I want to do. Don't take that in the wrong way, though; I'm not saying that you should just party your life away, or do bad things or break the law. That is not what I'm saying. I'm going to live a life where I will be happy. I'm going to get a job that will pay me a good salary. I'm not going to be in debt. I'm not going to stress out. I can go on vacations when I want to. I want to live a life where I will be happy.

I know many people who don't like their jobs. They don't like it because it's too stressful, they can't get out of debt, or other types of things, and they don't live a happy life. So, when I grow up, and get a nice steady job, I'm going to live debt-free. That's what I think a happy life means: to have a nice family and live a rich life. And I'm going to live my life to the fullest. How do you do that? I don't know how I'm going to do that, but I have a plan that I want to follow. If you want to live like that—being stuck at a desk answering other people's problems, while they live a happy life and you're just sitting there doing nothing and being all stressed out, and you consider that to be happy—then you go ahead and you do that, but I know I'm not going to be that person. I'm going to do whatever I want to. I'm going to go on a nice vacation with my family. I might be repeating myself here, but I'm just telling you that this is what living life to the fullest means. You don't have to sit at a desk and do stuff.

Things You Should Teach Your Teen

Notes

Notes

Notes

Notes

Chapter 4

How Teens Thrive in Their Everyday Life

Every day, over 3 billion people use the Internet. They can either communicate with someone else, search for things, or use it for their own entertainment. I use the Internet for all of these, and many more. Without the Internet, I believe that I would not be this far today. I'm going to be very honest with you; I use the Internet for pretty much everything I do. If I get a project, I automatically go to the Internet, and so will pretty much everybody else. Why do I go to the Internet though? I go to the Internet because I know it's quick and easy, and I can get done anything in the blink of an eye. So, how do I thrive in my everyday life, using the Internet? I thrive because it helps me to get my stuff completed on time. An example is my spelling. When I was in grades 4 to 7, I would use dictionary.com. I did not want to look through a dictionary for half an hour when I could just get it done in less than 10 minutes. Even though my teacher told me to use a dictionary, over and over and over again, I didn't, because I knew that I would get it done as quick as I could, and then I could do whatever I wanted to do.

In my class, everybody uses the Internet. Rarely will someone pick up a dictionary and look through it to find a word. Yes, I know using a dictionary is good for you, but it's not as quick as the Internet. The Internet is not just used for homework and completing assignments and things like that; It is used for people to connect with one another. All over the world, big companies such as Apple, Microsoft, Google, Facebook, and any others that you can think of, use the internet. A great example of a big company using the internet is Google. I know that pretty much every single person on this Earth has heard of Google. Google is the world's most used search engine, with over 3 billion online searches on a daily basis. That means pretty much every single day, 365 days a year, Google get 3 billion searches a day. Now, that is crazy.

As a teen, I will use the Internet to do pretty much anything I want to do. With a couple of clicks of the button, whatever I want to look up, it's right in front of me in less than a couple of seconds. As a teenager, I want to be honest; I don't really know what the Internet is. You might be wondering how I do not know what the Internet is. Most people believe that the Internet is the World Wide Web, or www. These are two different things. This might be a little boring for you, but read it; you might learn some stuff. World Wide Web was created by a person named Tim Berners-Lee. The Internet was created by Robert E Kahn and Vint Cerf. The Internet is a massive network that connects millions of computers together globally, forming a network in which any computer can communicate with another computer, as long as both are connected to the Internet. The World Wide Web is a way to access information over the Internet. World Wide Web is an information sharing model that was built on top of the Internet. Now I know that the Internet is not what I actually think it is, but I really use the World Wide Web. Teenagers use the World Wide Web for almost everything, including school.

As you read this, you may be thinking that teenagers hate school, and you know what? You are right. Most people, from a young age, hate school, because school is boring. What teens learn in school are actually lessons that will help them for the rest of their lives. Teachers ask us one question over and over again. What is that question? When are we ever going to use this? From my experience, my teacher said you will use this without you even knowing that you're using it. When I was in SK, my teacher made me trace letters that were on a piece of wood, but the letters had a rougher texture so I would know how to write it. At the time, I thought, "Why do I have to do this," and now I know why. Doing this, since I write cursive, made it easier for me to remember because I had been tracing the letters.

Some other things you learn in school is how to make the right type of friends. In high school, making friends is much easier than most people believe. My sister said, in high school, you can make friends by doing what you like. An example would be, if you like art; then join an art club or take an art class, and then talk to people in the club or class, and maybe, you might just make a friend. Not everyone is going to be nice to you. There will be people who may pick on you and bully you, but just push all those thoughts out of your head and live your life.

School also teaches you the basic life skills that you need to succeed in life, such as basic math, English, responsibilities, respect, and discipline. In school, many teenagers struggle in math. A great example of this is my sister. She has struggled her whole life with math. She has struggled so much that now she knows when she's doing something right and when she's doing something wrong. For the first time in her whole life, she finally understands math fully, and she taught a math class for the first time. She can now help other people who are struggling, better than the teachers, because she has been there before. At the end of the day, I believe that my sister is smarter than the kids who are top of the class, because they don't like to fail, and they lose out on the knowledge of doing a math question another way. I'm always hard on my sister because I want her to succeed, but without me knowing, my sister, Ra'eesa, was winning in her own way this entire time.

Tip for the parents out there: if your teen is struggling, then maybe you should step back and listen to what they have to say, and then tell them to keep on going, and that they can do it, no matter what. You should still put a little bit of pressure on them, but don't put too much pressure because then you can make them feel like they are failures. You should never do this because then they will never succeed. Once you have told them this, and you've listened to them, then rethink your strategy, and help them so they will succeed, no matter what.

In my school, we have something called mentorship. In mentorship, my partner and I go to another class, and we'll play games. We promote the book fair when it comes around, and we teach the younger kids. This teaches me how to become a leader. When my partner doesn't do things right, I take control. When the classroom gets crazy, I have learned that I am a leader. I give the younger kids a role model to look up. By doing all of this, it then brands myself as a leader—somebody you can trust, and someone you can give responsibilities to, and that you know will get it done. I do not just set a role model for the other kids; I'm a role model in my class for other people. Many people want to be a great leader, as I am in my class. I learned to be a good leader by doing extracurricular activities at my school, and out of school; and so far, they have been serving me well.

Every day, over the world, many teens do extracurricular activities. What are extracurricular activities? Many of you would probably say sports, art, and things like that. You are right, but what you probably don't know is that extracurricular activities are activities that fall outside of the school curriculum. Some extracurricular activities that many people do are student clubs, sports teams, volunteering, or even part time jobs. Why do teenagers do extracurricular activities? Many teenagers do extracurricular activities because it is an activity that they enjoy doing. When you do sports, what do you learn? Many of you might say that you get better at the sport, you get to meet new people, and whatever else you can think of at the moment. But when you do sports, it teaches you how to work together as a team, and it teaches you social skills. It also teaches you how to work with a team and how to progress with that team. One other thing that sports teaches is how to maintain patience and resilience at an intense and difficult time. Extracurricular activities also allow students to pursue interests outside of the academic system.

When teenagers do extra-curricular activities, it widens their social circle. It helps to build better time management, and if they are doing a sport, they also get healthier. When a teenager does extracurricular activities that they like, they get to enjoy it too. Like I said, it opens the social circle. Opening their social circle is a very good thing because they can interact with people who have the same interests as they do, and they can make new friends. How do extracurricular activities build better time management? When a teenager has a busy schedule with school and their job and things like that, when you add an extracurricular activity, their schedule gets really busy. So, what should they do? I would suggest that they create a schedule. Studies have shown that when a schedule gets really busy, and you add an extracurricular activity to it, they automatically organize and prioritize what they have to do.

Teenagers are Awesome

Notes

Notes

Teenagers are Awesome

Notes

Chapter 5

Why Teens Are So Awesome

Since the first human on earth, humans have evolved dramatically. Teenagers born in the early 2000s have evolved from the teens born in the 1980s. During your childhood, your brain hits a growth spurt, and by the age of six, your brain is already 90–95 % of an adult size brain. That just shows that having a big brain doesn't mean you are smarter. At the age of six, your brain is nowhere near the same development compared to an adult. During adolescence, your brain starts to fully develop because of a growth in synapses. You could say that our brain is at its highest peak. Your brain doesn't keep all the synapses because, if there are too much synapses, it can disrupt the connection within the cerebellum, and this could lead to autism. So what does your brain do? Your brain starts pruning away synapses. You might not understand, so let me tell you in an easier way. When your brain prunes away synapses, it is removing synaptic connections in your brain so that you don't get problems like autism.

Your prefrontal cortex hasn't fully developed until you reach your mid-20s. Teenage brains react different to certain situations, such as when a teenager is presented with something of a high reward—their brain gets more excited than when presented with something of low reward. In my own experience, this is true. An example is, when someone gives me a new pair of Jordan, LeBron, or any other type of basketball shoes, I get really excited. When you get excited, your brain releases some chemicals called endorphins, dopamine, serotonin, and oxytocin. These chemicals that the brain releases are responsible for happiness. If someone gives me a shirt with some animated thing on it, I won't get as excited because it's not something I like, so my brain won't release all these chemicals.

Why Teens Are So Awesome

As a teenager, I bring new ideas to the table that adults don't think of. I also bring solutions to the table that adults don't think about. Having the mind of a teen and the knowledge of an adult is the best thing ever. EVERY adult on earth was a teen at some time. They might not have been born during a time like this, but they were a teen during a time when something was evolving. I'm so happy to say that I was born during a time when everything was having a massive boom in technology. If it weren't for this, I think that I would not be the same because, as a teen, the technology has impacted by life dramatically.

As a teenager, every day, I have tons and tons of energy. So, what do I do? What I do to get rid of all the energy is to become active. Some ways to do this is by playing sports, such as basketball, soccer, baseball, hockey, football, etc., or going for bike rides, playing outside, or hiking; there are lots of things I do to get rid of my energy. In the winter time, when it's cold outside, some things that you can do are skiing, snowboarding, skating, or indoor swimming. If you're not one of those people who like to do sports, then you could maybe take cooking classes, join some clubs, or volunteer. Just be productive instead of just sitting in the house and playing games all day.

I feel that cooking is something that will help get rid of energy, and it will teach you how to survive by yourself when you go off to college or university. You won't have to eat junk all the time, and you can cook a healthy meal so you can stay fit and healthy. If you like playing sports, learning how to cook is essential if you want to live a healthy life and continue to play the sport. Cooking is also a great way to spend more time with your kids, and for you to build a bond with your team. When I'm in the kitchen with my mom, I help her cut up onions and peppers, and I help to prepare the table. By doing this, I create a stronger bond with her, and we end up loving each other so much. Cooking with my mom has influenced me in a great way because now I know how to cook food when she's not home, such as eggs, pancakes, and waffles—mostly breakfast foods, and some dinner food.

But the person who has helped me the most when I was cooking is my grandmother. My grandmother always cooks, and I'm always there standing next to her, observing, so I will know what to do next time she cooks a dish. Even though I want to help my grandmother, sometimes I don't want to interfere because she feels like I'm going to mess up the dish. In my opinion, my grandmother is one of the best cooks in the world that I know. In my opinion, my grandmother and grandpa are the best, and I'm about to tell you why. So, you already know that my grandma is a chef, but my grandpa, he's the one that makes the magic happen.

My grandpa loves gardening, so he plants all the vegetables and plants in our backyard, so then, when my grandma is ready to cook, she can grab the fresh and organic vegetables from our garden to put into our food—now isn't that just amazing? Speaking about gardening, that's another great way for teens to get rid of their anger and their energy. If your teen is depressed, or always angry, gardening has been scientifically proven to help humans relax; it reduces the amount of stress that they are going through. Gardening (this is a fun fact) has also been scientifically proven to help everything from coronary disease to cancer. With all this inspiration, I have learned to go big or go home.

Go big or go home—what does that mean? *Go big or go home* means to always go all out or don't try at all. That is my interpretation of *go big or go home*. Many people have different interpretations of this phrase. In this bit, I'm going to tell you why you should always aim high and never too low. When you're in a job, and let's just say you get a chance to ask your boss for a raise, how much are you going to ask for? Let's say you're making $1,000 a week. How will you ask for a raise? Are you going to be shy, and say, "Oh, you know, I just want a little bit more," or are you going to aim high and then go down low? So, from $1,000, are you going to go to $2,000, or are you going to stay at $1,500?

Go big or go home. It's not just about money; it can also be if you're going to say a speech or something. Something like that, you always want to do your best because, if you're not going to do your best, then don't do it at all. Whenever you are doing a speech, do your best, and talk about something that many adults are too afraid to talk about, which is something that teenagers do. As a teenager, I talk about things that many adults don't want to talk about, because we have a greater impact on the world then they have at the moment. So, when an adult sees that a young teenager is talking about something so big that nobody else wants to deal with it, you are going to be praised for what you have done. When I get offered something, I go big, and I don't go home. I always set my goal to be high because I'm not afraid of the consequences. I know, if I go higher, I can drop it to a lower number. Here's an example: I'm about to get a job, and the salary is $50,000.

Teenagers are Awesome

My boss asks me how much I would want. I might say $100,000. Now, if he says that's too high, then I could still drop it down to $90,000. If he said no, then I could say $80,000, then $70,000. Then, if he says yes... you see, I aimed high; then I brought it down low, and I still went pretty big, because I got $20,000 more than what I was offered.

Notes

Teenagers are Awesome

Notes

Why Teens Are So Awesome

Notes

Teenagers are Awesome

Notes

Chapter 6

How Teens Will Change the World

As a teenager, I want to change the world. I want to live in a world where everything is safe and nobody gets hurt—where there's no racism, and there's no difference between man and woman—everybody lives together in a happy world. As teenagers, we are the new generation. When your generation is dead, we will go on to change the world. We will break any social stereotypes. We are risk-takers. We will do whatever we need to do to live in a world where everybody is safe and nothing bad happens.

At the moment, the world we are living in is corrupted by both politics and the media. That's why, when I grow up, I'm going to change the world. I'm going to give people more opportunities. I'm going to lead the world into a new era, and so will every other teenager. When we get to the new world, there will be lots of technology, and we can use that to our advantage, because we have technology. Do not ask me about it—*cuz it is top secret.* This is just all my theories—just my opinions—so if any of this offends you, I'm sorry.

So, how are we *risk takers?* I'm a risk-taker: when I want something, I go for it, and I don't care what is in my way. I'm going to get it, and I don't care what the consequences are. I'm going to get what I want, and that is how I am a risk-taker. Teenagers are the exact same way. For example, when I want to make money, I do whatever I can to get it. I don't care if I have to be a little scamp or something. I still make money—more than anybody else—and that's what matters to me—*cuz I am a risk-taker.* I don't care what people think; I don't care about that as long as I'm happy. They might be saying that all that's a little selfish. I don't think so, because I'm a risk-taker; and I will lead the world into a new era.

How will we break from social stereotypes? I can't answer that question, but a great book that can is *Make My World a Better Place*, by Ra'eesa Baksh. This is a really good book that talks about racism, stereotypes, the media, corruption, and the government—all these types of things, this book will answer.

When we get to the new era, the teenagers of this generation will have broken off from the normal cycle. The normal cycle is being employed, doing something over and over, and just living a life where you work for somebody and you get paid. That is my interpretation of the normal cycle. I don't remember where I heard or saw this, but somebody said that when you break off from the normal cycle, you will go off onto a new path that will be much harder. It will be more difficult in other ways. That path doesn't get taken a lot, so it's going to be a lot harder to go through. When you take a new path, you'll jump to somewhere you've never been before, and you'll create new opportunities for other people to come join, so that you all can excel in your life. WI will influence people to take that path, and help these people through. If they want to stay with the normal cycle, I will let them stay. I'm not going to help them then, and even though that might sound a little harsh, they need to take that first step to do the right thing, and then I will help them.

An example is, when I was younger, I wanted to skateboard; but the first thing I had to do in order to learn was to get a skateboard. Someone wasn't going to just give me a skateboard; I had to know how to get that myself. That is taking the first step towards learning how to skateboard; and you have to do the same thing if you want to go off onto a new life path: you have to take the first step. Nobody's going to just hand you the way to success. You have to work for it, and you have to take the first step to succeed in life.

How do I create opportunities? I will create opportunities by creating a business. I've already told you that being the *norm* is bad, but if I create opportunities for people to work under me, that's like being the norm, right? But it's not, because if someone works under me, I will give them a job and educate them, and teach them in ways that they've never been taught before. Then I'll send them off onto a new life path. That is how I believe I'll treat opportunities for the future.

The last thing I want to say before you finish reading my book, is how I'm going to influence people. If you read my book, I probably influenced you to buy it, right? I probably said something that made you change your mind and buy my book, the same way that I will influence people on how to take the right path in life. It is the same way I got ahead in life—I influenced certain people that helped me get ahead. When I grow up, I'm going to tell people how to get on their life path. A lot of motivational speakers tell you to write down your goals. Listen to that advice, and try to achieve your goals. But the thing that they don't tell you is that you have to take the first step. They're not going to come to your house every morning and ask you what your goal is. It's up to you to do what you want.

Now, since you've reached the end of my book, I would like to say thank you for reading it, and I hope you learned a lot. Whatever you learned, I want you to take that into your life and use it.

How Teens Will Change the World

Notes

Teenagers are Awesome

Notes

Notes

Teenagers are Awesome

Notes

BONUS CHAPTER

What Do You Want To Be?

What do you want to be is a question that I'm guessing you have heard before? See when you are ages 3-9 this question is something that brings up our imagination. Now as a teen you and I are looking for a job. I'm not talking about working at McDonald, or another fast-food restaurant, I'm talking about a real job, like becoming a doctor, an engineer, something that. So today I'm going to give you some ideas of jobs that will help you in the long run. Also, now your parents won't have to bug you because you can say that you are looking in to it. The first job I recommend is a surgeon/doctor. A surgeon is a medical practitioner qualified to practice surgery. To become a surgeon, you are required to go to four years of undergraduate school, four years of medical school, and then 3-10 years of residency and fellowship training. Surgeons also have to continue their education throughout their job to maintain their license.

A surgeon makes roughly $252,910 - $525,000.

The surgeon that makes over half a million dollars is a cardiologist.

A cardiologist is a doctor who that deals with diseases and abnormalities in the heart. If you are think of being a doctor or surgeon, remember that you have to have a strong stomach for many of the things you are looking at. Things from Ischemic heart disease, to the cold and flu, and even some rare disease. The pay also varies from places. Number 2. An engineer. An engineer plays a very important role in our world. Without engineer our world would be in the stone age and I wouldn't have written this book. Let's take a look at what engineers do. When you wake up in the morning and you brush your teeth, shower, eat breakfast, and go to school either by car, bike, transit, something like that an engineer has touch at least 1 part of that transportation object. A car, an engineer such as a **mechanical** engineer. This engineer is responsible for most of the car. Just before the car is done an electrical engineer comes and wires your car so you can use the A/c and so you can listen to music on the radio.

An engineer's job is to help solve problems in our world. Math and science are their tools that they use to make work what it is today.

An engineer's salary can go from 50-200 grand. This all depends on what field you are in. I hope you become and engineer, so you can help this world. The last one I think you might like is working in construction management. Now this is a really cool job. Think about it when you see skyscraper around places you might think who built this. We'll let me tell. When you are going to build a building, you need a team of people. Not just construction workers but a team of leader so this project gets done. The first job you could do in construction management is becoming a project manager. The point of this job is to map out the enter process from start to finish. Next a design manager. The point of this job is to make the build look fabulous, functional, and tall. Next there is a quantity surveyor. A quantity surveyor figures out how much the project will cost the team. Then there is a Scheduler, this job is to find out how much time this project will take.

Then there is a contract manger. This job is very important because without this job, you wouldn't have the construction crew, plumber, painter, things like that because there is no contract. Then finally there is the construction crew that build the whole building. These are really cool jobs that can pay from 50-90 grand a year. Also when the building is finish you can say you built that.

What Do You Want To Be?

Notes

Teenagers are Awesome

Notes

What Do You Want To Be?

Notes

Notes

What Do You Want To Be?

Notes

Notes

About the Book

This book is to help parents and teens build a strong relationship with one another. Parents will understand how to communicate with their teens and how to address certain issues from a teenager's perspective. Teenagers will learn how to appreciate themselves and strive to become leaders of tomorrow. Remember, you are AWESOME!

About the Author

Ali Baksh is a 13-year- old who sees himself as a leader, a writer, and a trouble maker at times. He loves math, medical sciences, astronomy and helping others. Ali is a successful student who thinks outside the box and is very funny at times. He is very wise for his age and likes to share his opinions with others.